D0312291

LOOM
Magic Charms!

25 Cool Designs That Will Rock Your Rainbow

Becky Thomas & Monica Sweeney

Designs by Neary Alguard

Sky Pony Press
New York

Copyright © 2014 by Hollan Publishing, Inc.

Rainbow Loom® is a registered trademark and does not sponsor, authorize, or endorse this book.

Sky Pony Press books may be purchased in bulk at special discounts for sales promotion, corporate gifts, fund-raising, or educational purposes. Special editions can also be created to specifications. For details, contact the Special Sales Department, Sky Pony Press, 307 West 36th Street, 11th Floor, New York, NY 10018 or info@skyhorsepublishing.com.

Sky Pony® is a registered trademark of Skyhorse Publishing, Inc.®, a Delaware corporation.

Visit our website at www.skyponypress.com.

10 9 8 7 6 5 4 3 2

Library of Congress Cataloguing-in-Publication Data is available on file.

Cover design by Owen Corrigan
Cover photo credit Hollan Publishing, Inc.

ISBN: 978-1-63220-259-8
Ebook ISBN: 978-1-63220-260-4

Printed in the United States of Ameica

CONTENTS

ACKNOWLEDGMENTS

We'd like to thank our wonderful editor Kelsie Besaw and Sara Kitchen, who again helped us to get this book out in record speed! We would also like to thank everyone at Skyhorse for continuing to do a fantastic job with this series. Thank you to Bill Wolfsthal, Tony Lyons, and Linda Biagi for putting it all together and giving us this opportunity. We'd also like to thank Holly Schmidt for her unending support and Allan Penn for his excellent photography.

Finally, we'd like to thank all of our models, Alden Glovsky, Nathaniel Stanwood, Owen Schmidt, Christa Coffey, Leah Coffey, and Lucy Bartlett, who lent their smiling faces to our book.

GLOSSARY

Here is a list of some of the terms we use when explaining how to do each project. Getting to know them will help you speed through all these great designs!

hook: The hook is the off-white, hook-shaped utensil that is provided in the packaging of your loom. This is used to move rubber bands from their pegs instead of your fingers.

c-clip: A c-clip, as its name suggests, is a small, clear clip shaped like a "c" that we use to hold rubber bands together. C-clips are often the last step in a project. Some rubber band kits come with s-clips instead; you can use those the same way you use c-clips.

threading: To thread beads onto your project, wrap a thin piece of wire—such as a stripped twist-tie—around a single band. Add the beads onto the wire from the other end, and then slide them onto the band.

Set up your loom square: When all the columns are evenly set on the loom; no column of pegs is set forward or backward.

offset: When columns in the loom are not square. For example, when the outside columns are set evenly and the middle column is set one peg closer to you.

Making a chain or **"knitting":** To make a chain for arms or feet, wrap a single band around your hook three or four times so it looks like a knot. Attach a double band to the end of the hook, and slide the knot onto this double band. Move everything back onto the shaft of the hook. Continue this process of adding double bands to the chain until you have the desired length.

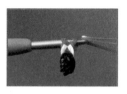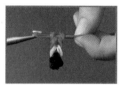

Holding bands: Holding bands are placed across the rows of your charms before you loop the project. They help to keep all the bands in your designs in the right shape. Do not loop holding bands: when you loop your other bands, pull them through the holding bands as you would with any cap bands.

Doubling: To double a rubber band, fold it onto itself before placing it onto the loom or hook. This makes the band extra tight. When a project calls for doubled bands, the instructions will often say to wrap the band around your hook twice before placing it on the loom; this is an easy way to attach a tight doubled band to multiple pegs. Do not confuse this with a double band: two single bands placed on the loom together.

Double band: Two single rubber bands placed onto the loom together.

How to "Loop" your project back: When you have finished putting down all your rubber bands on the loom, there is one more step before you can remove your project from the loom. This step connects your bands to each other instead of just to the loom.

To Loop Your Project:

1. Start at the peg indicated in the instructions; usually it is the last or second-to-last peg in your project or the peg where you have put a cap band.

2. Use your plastic hook tool and slide it into the hollow space in the middle of the peg to grab the top un-looped band on the peg.

3. Then pull the band up and off the peg, pulling it through any cap bands or any looped bands stacked above it.

4. Attach the band on your hook to the peg where the other end of the same band is still attached. If there is more than one band, loop all the bands on a peg before you move on to loop the next peg.

5. Pegs are typically looped in the opposite order from how you laid them out on the loom, but be sure to follow any specific instructions for the project you are working on.

6. When you have finished looping your project, you should have a few loose loops remaining on the last peg on the loom. You need to secure those loops by tying a band around them or using a c-clip or your project will unravel!

T-Rex

For the fiercest of loom projects, meet the T-Rex! This Tyrannosaurus looks just like the real thing, but luckily for you, we are not in the Cretaceous Period and he is not made of sharp claws and teeth. This project has a lot of steps for his many different body parts, so just be careful to follow all of the steps in order.

Difficulty level: **Hard**

You need:

1 loom • 2 hooks • dark green bands • red bands • white bands • black bands

Set up your loom offset so that the center column is one peg farther from you.

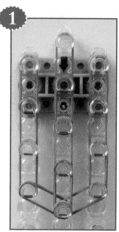

1. First you will make the T-Rex's mouth. For the top jaw, lay out the figure shown using green double bands. Attach a cap band at the bottom center peg.

2. Using single bands that have been "doubled," or wrapped once on themselves, lay out two triangular holding bands. To make his nostrils, wrap two separate single bands around your hook several times. Slide both of them onto another single green band and attach this to your loom at the fourth outside pegs.

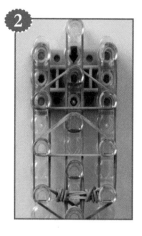

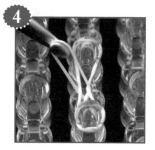

3. For the teeth, you will attach a single band to the loom, wrapping it in a figure eight.

4. Using your hook, take the bottom band on one side and loop it over the peg to the center of the band. Do this again on the opposite side.

5. Your teeth should look like little knots. Repeat this process eleven more times for a total of twelve teeth.

6. Attach the teeth to the second, third, and fourth pegs on the left and right sides of the figure. Starting from the

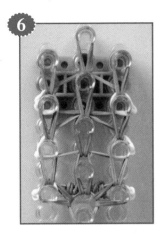

cap band at the bottom, loop the jaw back to the top of the loom. Before removing from the loom, secure the top three bands temporarily on a holding hook or with c-clips. Set aside.

7. For the bottom part of the jaw, attach green double bands to your loom in the figure shown. Note that the diagonal bands have been attached after the band between pegs 1 and 2 in the outside columns, but before the outside bands from pegs 2 to 3. Fill in the center column last and finish with a cap band.

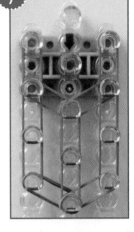

8. Attach three single holding bands to the project. These bands will be "doubled," meaning that they have been wrapped once on themselves so they are tight. Add the remaining teeth to the second, third, and fourth pegs in the left and right columns.

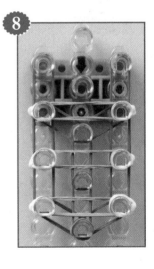

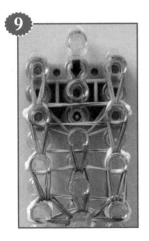

9. Starting from the cap band, carefully loop the bands back to the pegs where they started. Like the top part of the jaw, secure the top of the project with a holding hook or c-clips, remove from the loom, and set aside.

10. For the legs, attach green double bands to 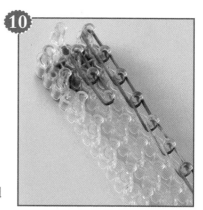 the loom for seven rows. Note the fifth and sixth bands have been "doubled" to make them tight. Attach a cap band to the bottom peg. Add two bands just before the top of the center column—this will help make the thigh look bigger.

11. Before looping the legs back, you will need to make the T-Rex's claws by creating tiny single chains. Wrap a white band around your hook several times.

12. Slide the white band onto a green band that has been "doubled" or wrapped once on itself to make it tight. Add two more of these green bands until you have small claws.

13. You will need to create three claws for each foot and arm, for a total of twelve claws.

14. Attach three of the claws to the bottom of the leg. Attach a "doubled" holding band between the third peg in the center column and the second peg in the right-hand column. Begin looping the bands back to the pegs where they started. After you've reached the fourth peg from the top, loop the band diagonally to the bands in the center column. Finish looping the center column, and then return to finish looping the right-hand column. Secure both of these top loops with a holding hook or a c-clip and set aside. Make two legs.

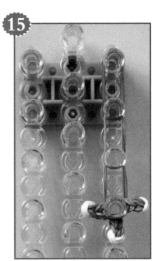

15. For the T-Rex's short arms, create a single chain using three bands. The first band will be a double band, and the second two will be single bands that have been "doubled" so they are tight. Attach the three claws to the bottom peg and add a cap band.

16. Starting from the cap band, loop the bands in the arm back to where they started. Secure the arm on a holding hook or with a c-clip and set aside. Make two arms total.

17. For the tail, lay out the figure shown using green single bands on the outside columns and double bands on the inside column. Attach the bands in the center column first, followed by the outside columns. Note that the diagonal bands stretch an extra peg-length. Finish the end of the tail with a cap band.

18. Add five triangular holding bands that have been "doubled" and one regular holding band at the bottom of the tail, which will also be "doubled."

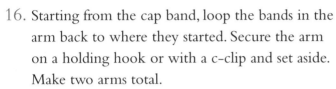

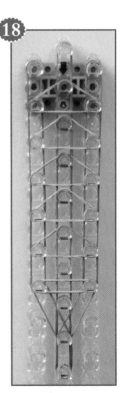

19. Starting from the cap band at the bottom, loop the bands in your project back to the pegs where they started. Secure the tops of the project and set aside.

20. For the T-Rex's head, lay out the small hexagon shown using single bands. Fill in the center column after you have laid out the hexagon.

21. Thicken the neck by attaching a double band between the second and third pegs in the center column. Continue the figure in the arrangement shown—make sure to add the double band in the center column after the first set of diagonal bands but before the second set of diagonal bands.

22. Finish the torso by making a large hexagon. The outside columns will be single bands and the center column will be double bands.

23. For the eyes, wrap a black band around your hook several times. Slide it onto a "doubled" red band. Once you have two eyes, slide these onto a single green band. Attach the eyes across the second outside pegs, then attach a single triangular holding band. Lay out three more triangular holding bands across the torso.

24. Carefully attach the tail, legs, and arms to the T-Rex's body. Note that the arms attach to the diagonal shoulder bands—so you will wait to add

them until you reach the shoulder bands in your looping process. Loop all of the bands up to the face, then stop just before the top so you can add the mouth.

25. Attach the bottom part of the jaw to the second outside pegs.

26. Attach the top part of the jaw to the same row, though this time you will be attaching the three bands over each peg in the row. This part will have a lot of bands, so you may find it easiest to loop the face bands as you attach each part of the top jaw to secure it. Once the jaws are secure, finish looping the rest of the

project and secure the head at the top before removing the project from the loom.

27. Once the T-Rex is off the loom, you may need to fiddle with the bands to get his eyes out front or to make him sit the way you like.

TOP HAT

Fancy up your loom charms with this great top hat! Use it as a charm to dangle from a keychain, or put it on top of your favorite loom animals! This project is quick and easy and makes a great accessory!

Set up your loom square. All bands will be
double bands.

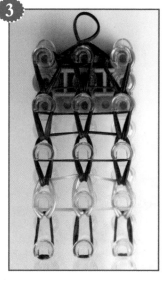

1. Lay out the figure of black and gold double
   bands, as shown.

2. Attach single black holding bands over the
   second and third rows, and then attach a
   single gold holding band over the third row.
   Attach black cap bands to each of the three
   bottom pegs.

3. Loop the bands back to the pegs where
   they started, doing the outside columns
   first. Loop the horizontal bands in the

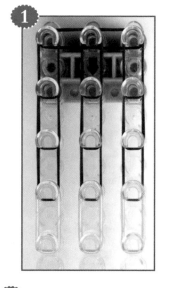

   first row to the center,
   then loop the middle
   column. Attach a c-clip
   or a band to the top of
   the project. Remove the
   hat from the loom and
   set aside.

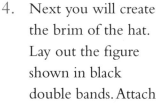

4. Next you will create
   the brim of the hat.
   Lay out the figure
   shown in black
   double bands. Attach
   a single cap band to the corner of the project
   where you placed the last set of bands.

5. Take the top of the hat and put it upside down into the gap in the
   loom. Attach each of the black loops in the hat to the corresponding

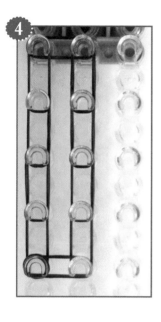

middle pegs (each loop should attach to two pegs).

6. Starting with the cap band in the brim and moving to the peg in the opposite column, loop the bands back to the pegs where they started. Loop the two columns going from bottom to top (do not loop in a square).

7. Attach a single band or a c-clip to tie off the project. Gently remove from the loom.

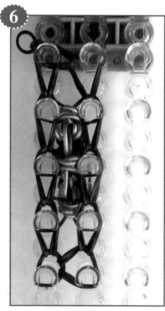

SUNFLOWER

This sunny flower will brighten your day! This project is simple to put together, but because the bands are tight, it does take a little extra concentration to make sure they don't snap. If you would like to make a bigger flower, simply replace the single bands with double bands throughout the project.

Difficulty level: **Medium**

You need:

1 loom • 2 hooks • green bands • black bands • yellow bands

Set up your loom offset so that the center column is one peg farther away from you. All bands are single bands that have been "doubled," or wrapped once on themselves.

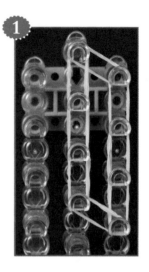

1. For the sunflower petals, lay out the trapezoid in the photo using single bands that have been doubled.

2. Attach two triangle holding bands, as shown. Both of these will be single bands that have been "doubled." Attach a cap band to the bottom right-hand corner of the figure.

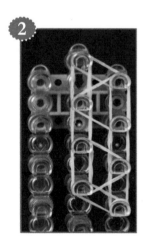
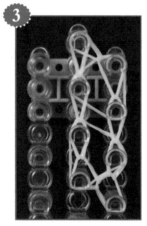

3. Starting from the cap band, loop the left side of the petal up to the top peg. Return to the cap band and loop the right side of the petal, finishing at the top of the loom. Secure the top of the project on a holding hook or with a c-clip.

4. Repeat this five more times for a total of six petals, and set them aside for later.

5. For the leaf that will go on the stem, lay out a slightly smaller version of

the petals you just made. Similarly, these green bands will all be single bands that have been "doubled."

6. Attach a triangular holding band to the petal. This will be a single band that has been "doubled." Add a cap band to the bottom peg on the right-hand side of the project.

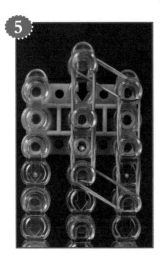
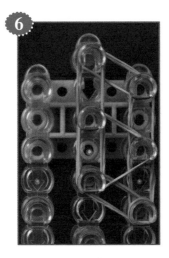
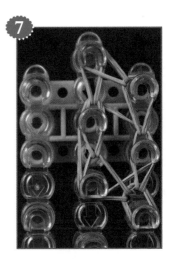

7. Starting from the cap band, loop the left side of the project back up to the top of the loom. Return to the cap band and loop the remaining pegs on the right side of the loom, finishing at the top peg. Secure the leaf and set it aside for later.

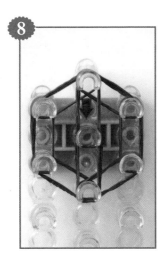

8. For the eye of the sunflower, lay out a hexagon shape using black single bands that have been "doubled." Attach the ones in the center after you have laid out the hexagon.

9. Using a single black band that has been "doubled," attach a triangular holding band to the center of the hexagon.

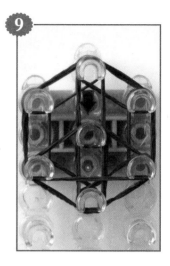

10. Lay out the stem of the flower using green single bands that have been "doubled," as shown. Attach a cap band to the last peg in the stem.

11. Carefully attach the green leaf to the stem, as well as five of the six sunflower petals. Leave the center peg at the bottom of the flower free for the moment.

12. Starting with the cap band, loop the bands back to the pegs where they started, finishing at the top of the stem that connects to the flower.

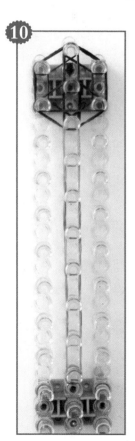

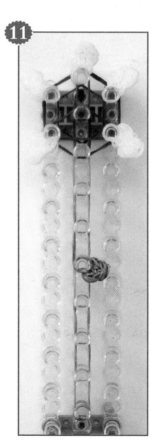

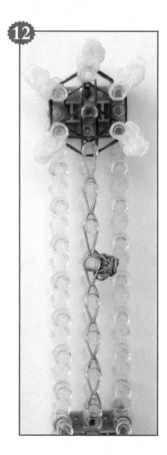

13

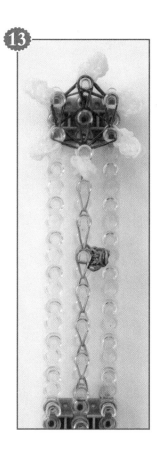

13. Attach the remaining petal to the center bottom peg in the flower (just at the top of the stem). Loop the black bands back to the pegs where they started. Since there are so many bands, it may be helpful to use another hook to release the tension as you go.

14. Secure the project and gently remove from the loom.

FLiP FLOPS

Get ready for beach weather with these cool sandals! This super easy project is great for jewelry—just attach the top of the flip flops to earring hooks or to a funky bracelet.

Difficulty level: **Easy**

You need:

1 loom • 1 hook • purple bands • white bands

Set up your loom offset, so that the center column is one peg away from you. All bands will be single bands that have been "doubled," or wrapped once on themselves so they are taut.

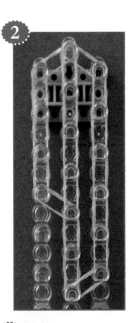

1. Lay out the beginning of your flip flop in the formation shown. Make sure you are using single bands that have been "doubled."

2. Add to the formation by attaching six more bands down the center column. Connect this column to the right-hand side with a diagonal band.

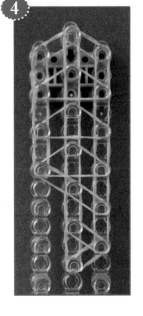

3. Lay out five holding bands: three triangle-shaped and two smaller ones. All of these should be single bands that have been "doubled." Attach a cap band to the bottom of the project.

4. Loop the bands back to the pegs where they started. Make sure to start with the bands closest to the top of the pegs. Loop the center column only part way.

5. Finish looping the rest of the center column. Doing this last will help hold the project together.

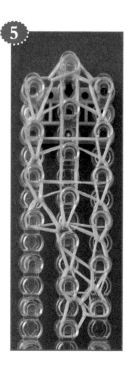

6. Take two single white bands and wrap them in slipknots at either side of the flip flops.

7. For added effect, twist the white bands several times before securing them at the top of the sandal with another rubber band.

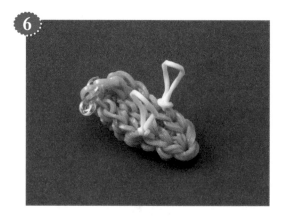

DOLLAR SiGN

Money isn't everything, but this rubber band dollar sign hits the jackpot. This project is fun and simple, but just be careful to follow the layout and looping instructions in the correct order.

Difficulty level: **Medium**

You need:

1 loom • 1 hook • rubber bands

Set up your loom offset so that the center column is one peg farther away from you than the others. All the bands are double bands (two rubber bands used as one).

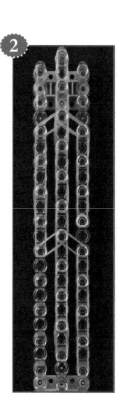

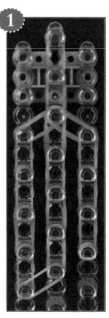

1. Lay out the first figure shown using double bands. Start by adding the first two double bands in the center column. Next, branch out to the outside columns, laying the bands from the top down. Add the center column, and then connect the center column to the left column with a double band.

2. Continue down the dollar sign, forming the center column and the bottom right side of the "S."

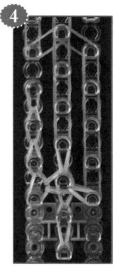

3. Lay out the rest of the "S," making sure to move clockwise as if you were writing the "S" with a pen. Add the bottom two double bands to finish the center column. Attach cap bands to both ends of the "S," as well as at the bottom of the dollar sign.

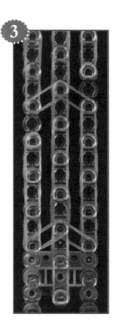

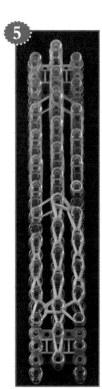

4. Starting with the cap band at the tail of the dollar sign, loop the first two bands back to the pegs where they started. Then go to the end of the S, and begin looping back those bands. This part of the "S" will feel funny to loop because bands are not ordinarily laid out from bottom to top, but this is okay. When looping the band that connects the center column to the right column, make sure you are moving counterclockwise.

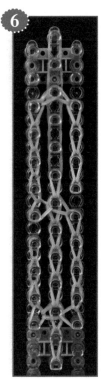

5. Continue looping the bands up to the center of the dollar sign, looping the right-hand column second.

6. Continue clockwise up the rest of the left side of the "S" to the center column. Then, starting from the cap band at the tip of the "S" on the right-

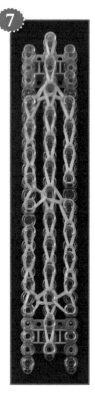

hand side, loop the bands back up to the center column.

7. Finish looping the center column all the way up to the top of the dollar sign. Tie off the top of the project with a c-clip or an additional single band. Gently remove from the loom.

APPLe

The stem and leaf of this project are both made using all doubled bands, meaning they are extra tight. When looping, you'll want to be careful so you don't break any bands or your hook!

Difficulty level: **Medium**

You need:

1 loom • 1 hook (use a metal hook if you have one) • red bands •
green bands • brown bands

1. Wrap a single brown band around your hook twice, then attach it from the second to the third peg in the left column. Repeat to continue laying out the stem as shown using tight doubled bands.

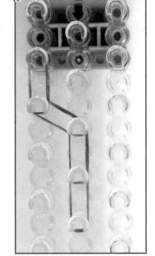

2. Lay out your apple's leaf shape using tight doubled bands. Start at the fourth middle peg and lay out two sets of green single bands, doubled, down the middle column, then attach another doubled green band from the first peg on the right to the second middle peg. Go back to the fourth middle peg and lay out the right half of the leaf shape, ending on the first peg on the right.

3. Place two doubled green bands across your leaf shape as holding bands. Wrap a single green band three or four times around the first peg on the right as a cap band.

4. Using double red bands, lay out your apple shape. Lay out the left side, starting at the sixth and ending on the ninth middle peg, then lay out the right side.

5. Take two red bands and wrap them around your hook twice, then attach them from the sixth to the seventh middle peg. Repeat twice more down the middle of your apple shape.

6. Attach holding bands to your apple shape. Take two red bands and attach them to the center of the apple in a triangle shape. Attach a single band across the row above the triangle and another across the row below. Wrap a single red band around the bottom middle peg of your apple three or four times as a cap band.

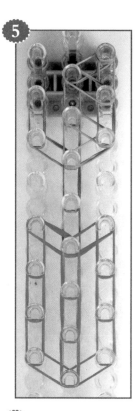

7. Using single bands, lay out a trapezoid shape below your apple. Layout the left side, then the right side. Wrap a single band around the last peg in the right column as a cap band. Wrap a single red band around your hook twice and attach it to the trapezoid in a triangle shape as a holding band.

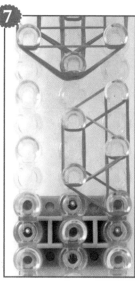

8. Loop your extra piece, looping each side out from the cap band and ending on the peg where you started.

9. Remove your extra piece from the loom and attach it to the side of your apple shape, placing the loose loops onto the top corner peg and the cap band end onto the third peg down. Make the other extra piece in the same way, and attach it to the other side of the apple.

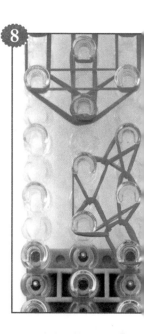

10. Begin looping your apple shape: Start at the cap band and loop up the four pegs in the middle column. Then loop the outside columns to the same last peg. When you have looped all the red bands, loop the first doubled brown band. Loop the leaf

shape next; you will be looping backwards for some of the bands. Loop the peg with the cap band, then loop out in both directions to end on the fourth middle peg where it attaches to the stem.

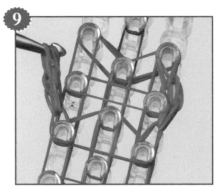

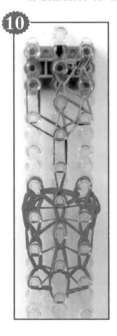

11. Finish looping your stem, working your way up until you have looped all the bands on your loom. Secure the final loose bands with a single brown band pulled in a slip knot.

12. Remove your apple from the loom.

TREBLE CLEF

Make beautiful music with this multicolored symbol! This is built all with double bands, so it's extra sturdy.

Set up your loom offset with the middle column
pulled away from you one peg.

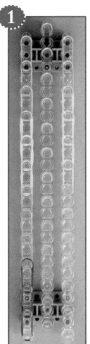

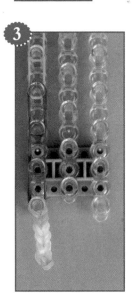

1. Lay a line of double bands down
    the left column, then lay a line of
    double bands halfway down the
    right column. If you are making
    your treble clef rainbow-colored,
    match the colors in the example,
    laying out orange, then yellow,
    then green, then blue bands on
    the right, and green then yellow
    bands on the left. Wrap a green
    band around the last peg in the
    right column three or four times
    as a cap band.

2. Loop the bands in your right
    column.

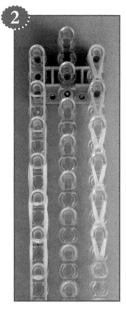

3. Remove the bands from the right
    column, and carefully place the
    loose loops from the end onto the
    last peg in the left column.

4. Loop your left column, treating
    the chain you just added as a cap
    band. Remove your long chain
    from the loom and set aside
    for now.

5. Using purple bands, lay a line
    of double bands down the left

column, ending on the sixth peg. Wrap a blue band around the sixth peg three or four times as a cap band.

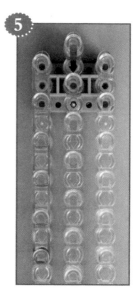

6. Loop your row as usual. Remove your chain from the loom and set aside.

7. Using double bands, lay a line of red bands down the middle column from the first to the fourth peg. Starting at the first and ending on the fourth middle peg, lay out a trapezoid shape to the right using red and orange bands. Then lay a line of bands down the middle column, starting at the fourth middle peg and continuing to the end of the loom. Follow the color changes of the example if you are making your treble clef rainbow-colored.

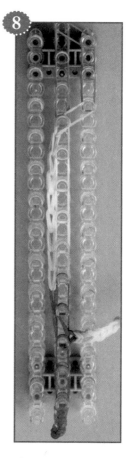

8. Attach the chains you had set aside. Place the purple chain onto the last middle peg. For

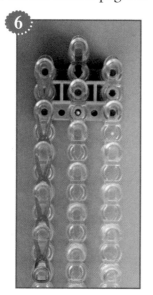

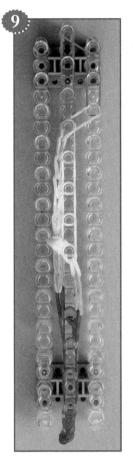

the longer chain, attach the orange end to the fourth middle peg, then find the eleventh stitch in the chain (counting the orange stitch), and loop it onto the third peg from the end.

9. Find the third stitch from the end of your same long chain, and attach it to the sixth peg from the end. Make sure you are laying the added chain parts down as shown so that your treble clef is shaped correctly.

10. Loop your treble clef shape as usual. Secure the last loops with a red single band pulled into a slipknot; do not pull the knot too tight or it will mess up your treble clef shape.

BANANA

This may just be the easiest charm there is! With just a few rubber bands and a simple banana shape, this light snack will be at your loom monkey's side in no time!

Difficulty level: **Easy**

You need:

1 loom • 1 hook • yellow bands • 2 brown or green bands

Set up your loom offset so the center column is one peg further away from you.

1. Lay out the banana shape shown, using single yellow bands that have been "doubled," or that have been wrapped once on themselves.

2. Add a brown cap band to the bottom right corner of the banana.

3. Using more single bands that have been "doubled," lay out holding bands to make the project tight. Notice that the holding bands in the top left corner look like a triangle.

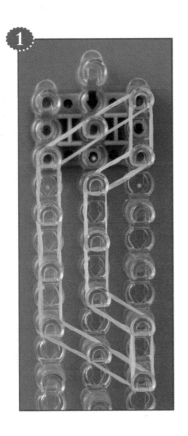 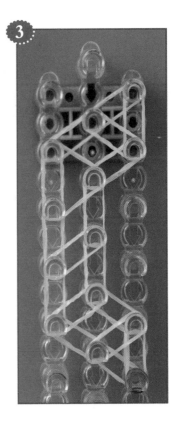

4. Starting from the brown cap band, loop the bands back to the pegs where they started. Start with one side of the project until you reach the end of the banana, and then go back and do the other side until you reach the end of the banana.

5. Tie off the project with a brown or green rubber band and gently remove from the loom.

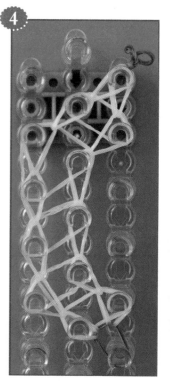

GiRAFFe

Y ou can replace any of your orange bands with brown bands to make spots, like we've done for this example. Make sure to work slowly when looping bands that have been doubled; they are extra tight, so be careful you don't break the bands or your hook!

Difficulty level: **Medium**

You need:

1 loom • 1 hook • orange bands • brown bands •
white bands • black bands

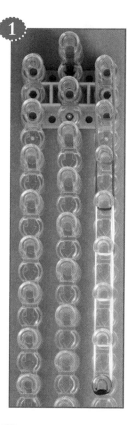

To Make the Legs:

1. Attach three orange bands from the first to the second peg in the right column. Continue laying a line of bands down that column, laying down two sets of double orange bands. Then wrap a white band around your hook twice and attach it from the fourth to the fifth peg. Lay out three more white bands this way. Wrap a black cap band around the last peg (the eighth peg) three times.

2. Starting at the peg where you placed the cap band, loop the bands in your leg. Remove the leg from the loom and set aside. Repeat to make four total legs.

To Make the Horns:

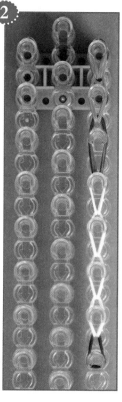

1. Wrap an orange band around your hook twice, then connect it to the first and second pegs in the left column. Repeat and attach the doubled orange band to the second and third pegs. Wrap a white cap band around the third peg three times.

2. Loop your horn as usual. Pull two orange bands through the

final loose loop to secure it, then remove the horn from your loom, keeping the double orange bands on your hook. Repeat to make your second horn, and leave it on your hook as well.

To Make Your Giraffe:

1. Attach the double orange bands from one of your horn pieces to the first middle and first left pegs. Attach the double bands from the other horn to the first middle and first right pegs.

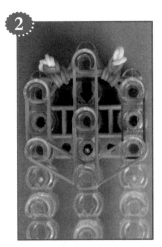

2. Using brown and orange double bands, lay out a small hexagon shape for your giraffe's head, starting where you laid out the giraffe's horns. Lay double orange bands down the middle of the small hexagon shape.

3. Lay out your giraffe's neck. Attach double orange bands from the third to the fourth middle peg. Attach a single orange band to the third middle peg and connect it to the left. Repeat and connect it to the right. Continue to lay double bands down the center and single bands down the outside columns, ending on the ninth peg.

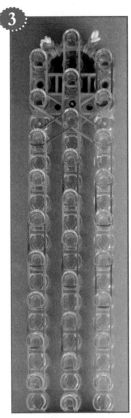

4. Lay out your giraffe's body: attach double orange bands to the ninth middle peg, and connect them to the left. Repeat and connect to the right. Lay double

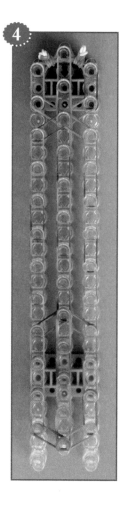

bands down the center column to the end and down the outside columns to the second to last peg. Close off your body shape by connecting double bands from the second to last outside pegs to the last middle peg. Wrap a cap band around the last middle peg three or four times.

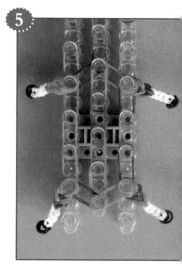

5. Attach your giraffe's legs. Connect the front legs to the outside columns five pegs from the end. Attach the back legs to the outside columns two pegs from the end.

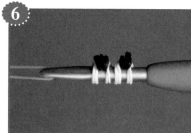

6. Make your giraffe's eyes. Wrap a black band around your hook four times. Double a white band onto itself and thread the black band onto the doubled white band. Put both ends of the white band onto the hook. Leaving your first eye on the hook, repeat to make the second. Stretch a single orange band between the hook and your finger and thread the eyes onto this. Leave it on your hook or set it aside for now.

7. Make your giraffe's ears. Wrap an orange band around your hook four times, then stretch double orange bands between your hook and your fingers

and thread the wrapped band onto it. Repeat to make the second ear.

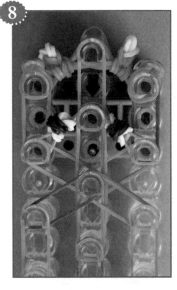

8. Attach your eyes and ears, as shown. Pull the middle of the "eye" band over the second middle peg, making sure to push the eyes to either side.

9. Lay "holding bands" across the whole shape. Wrap a single orange band around your hook twice and stretch it across the second row in a triangle shape. Repeat to lay triangle shapes down the whole body shape, as shown. In the eighth row, pull the holding band into a diamond shape. Wrap a single orange band around your hook twice and place the band across the third row. Place single bands in triangle shapes across the two rows between your giraffe's legs; do not double them.

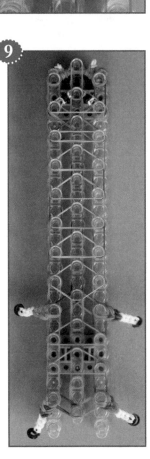

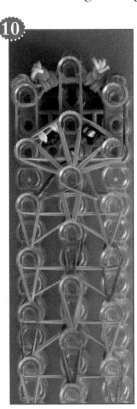

10. Starting at the peg where you placed your cap band, begin looping your giraffe shape. Loop as usual all the way up to the "chin" peg (the third middle peg). Once you have looped the chin peg, you will add additional bands for the giraffe's snout.

11. Push the bands of your giraffe's head down the pegs. Attach double white bands from the second to the third and the third to the

fourth middle pegs. Wrap a white band around your hook and attach it from the second to the third peg on the right. Repeat on the left. Place a doubled white band from the third outside peg to the fourth middle peg on either side to close your snout shape. Add holding bands by wrapping a band around your hook twice and attaching it to the third row in a triangle shape. Wrap a white band around your hook three times, and attach it to the second row (you can loop it twice if three times is too tight). Wrap a white band around the fourth middle peg three times for a cap band.

12. Loop the remaining bands of your giraffe. Pull double orange bands through the final loose loops and tie a slip knot to secure them. Remove your giraffe.

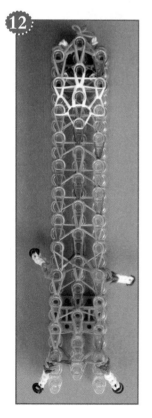

ELEPHANT

This is one pachyderm that won't leave peanuts all over your bedroom! Because you need to attach the ear to your elephant at specific points, the ear is laid out in a strange order; make sure to read the instructions carefully!

Difficulty level: **Easy**

You need:

1 loom • 1 hook • purple bands • light purple bands • pink bands • blue bands • white bands

To Make the Ears:

1. Use single purple bands to lay out the ear shape. Start at the fifth peg on the right and lay a line of single bands up the column, ending on the first middle peg. Starting at the first middle peg, lay out a trapezoid shape in the left column, ending on the fifth middle peg. Attach a single band from the fifth middle peg to the fifth peg on the left, then lay out diagonal bands from there to the sixth peg on the right. Lay a single band from the sixth to the fifth left peg to close the shape.

2. Lay out single bands in a trapezoid shape to make the extra piece for your ear. Lay out each half starting from the middle peg just below your ear shape. Wrap a single band around the eleventh middle peg three or four times as a cap band. Lay connector bands across the shape as shown.

3. Loop the extra piece, starting at the cap band and looping both sides back to the seventh middle peg.

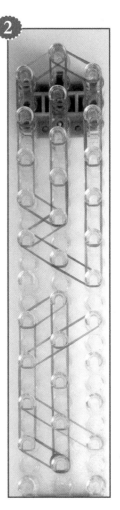

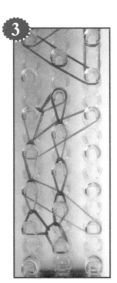

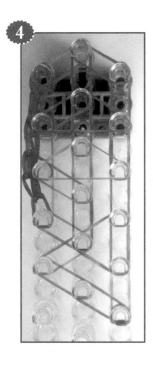

4. Carefully remove the extra piece, holding it by the cap band and by the loose loops from the other end. Place the extra piece onto the left column of the ear, attaching the cap band to the fourth peg, and the loose loops to the first peg. Attach the connector bands to the second and fourth middle pegs. Attach a cap band to the bottom right peg. Attach a single purple holding band to the second row in a triangle shape. Attach a second holding band, doubled, to the third row. Double a single purple band, and attach it to the fourth and fifth right pegs and fifth middle peg in a triangle shape.

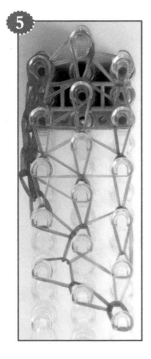

5. Starting at your cap band, loop your elephant's ear shape. Loop from the cap band up the right column to the second peg, then stop. From the cap band, loop the three bands going to the left, ending on the middle peg. Loop the rest of the middle column, then go back to the fifth middle peg and loop the left column, working your way around the outside of the ear in a clockwise direction until you reach the second peg in the right column. Secure the loose loops on that second peg, and remove your ear from the loom. Repeat to make your second ear.

To Make the Legs and Trunk:

1. To make your elephant's foot on the hook, wrap two light purple bands around your hook three times, then thread them onto a double purple band. Leave the foot on your hook. For the trunk, wrap a purple and pink band around your hook. Take two purple bands and double them, then thread the pink and purple loops onto the doubled bands.

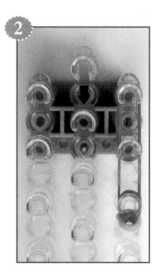

2. Lay a line of double bands down from the first to the third peg. Place your foot onto the third peg as a cap band. For the trunk, wrap your double bands around your hook twice before placing them on the loom, to make them extra tight.

3. Loop your chain back as usual. Carefully remove your leg from the loom and set it aside so that it doesn't unravel. To remove your trunk, pull a single purple band through the loose loops in a temporary slipknot. Make four total legs and one trunk this way.

To Make the Body:

1. Using double purple bands, lay out a small hexagon shape onto the loom. Lay double bands down the middle of the shape. Lay out a second small hexagon shape for the elephant's body. Lay double bands down the middle of that hexagon as well.

2. To make the eyes, wrap a blue band around your hook three times, then wrap a single white band around the blue band, wrapping it twice on either side. Repeat to make a second eye on the hook. Thread both eyes onto a single purple band. Place your eyes across the second row, with the middle of the band pulled over the second middle peg.

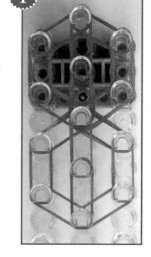

3. Attach your ears by placing the loose loops onto the first outside pegs. Undo the slipknot from your trunk and attach it using the single purple band. Attach your elephant's back legs to the fourth outside pegs.

4. Place a single band around the second row in a triangle shape as a holding band. Attach a second holding band across the fourth row in a triangle shape pointing in the other direction. Wrap a single band around the fifth peg three or four times as a cap band.

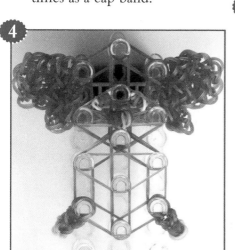

5. Begin looping your elephant, starting at the cap band. Loop the outside columns until you reach the third peg. When you loop from the third outside peg to the third middle (the neck peg), put one of the remaining legs onto your hook, and slide it onto the band before you place it onto the middle peg. Do the same on the other side to attach the other leg.

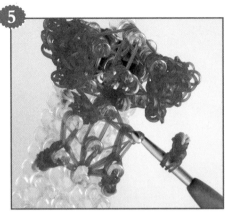

6. Loop the rest of your elephant shape. Secure the final loose loops with a single band pulled into a slipknot.

7. Remove your elephant from the loom.

FANCY FOX

This fox doesn't say much, but he'll make an excellent (and super cute) addition to your charm collection. Some of the bands in this project are stretched very tightly, so be extra careful when you're looping these.

Difficulty level: **Medium**

You need:

1 loom • 1 hook • orange bands • white bands • black bands • blue (or other eye color) bands

Set up your loom offset, with the middle column pulled one peg up.

To Make the Ears:

1. Lay a single orange band across the first row in a triangle shape. Attach single orange bands from the first to the second peg in each outside column. Wrap an orange band around your hook twice and place it over the third middle peg in a triangle shape. Attach a single white band from the first to the second middle peg. Pull your doubled orange band onto the second middle peg in a diamond shape. Wrap a black cap band around the third middle peg three or four times.

2. Begin looping your ear: grab the top strand of your doubled band. Very slowly, pull the strand up through the cap band and loop it onto the second peg on the right. Pull the other strand to the second left peg in the same way. Loop the outside orange bands and white band as usual. Loop the second orange triangle from the first outside pegs onto the first middle peg. Secure the loose bands and set aside. Make your second ear the same way.

To Make the Legs:

1. Lay out two sets of double orange bands down the right column. Wrap a black band around your hook twice, then stretch it from the third to the fourth peg. Repeat and attach it from the fourth to the fifth peg. Wrap a black cap band around the fifth peg three or four times.

2. For the front legs, loop the bands back as usual. For the back legs, place double orange bands from the second to the third middle peg.

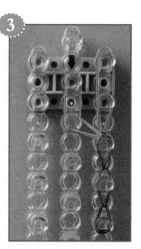

3. For your leg shape, when you loop your orange bands from the third peg, loop them onto the third middle peg. Loop the rest of the bands as usual. Remove the leg from the loom, secure the loose bands with a spare hook, and set aside. Remember to secure both sets of loose loops from the back leg pieces.

To Make the Tail:

1. Attach a single orange band to the first middle peg and connect it to the right. Repeat and connect it to the left. Lay a line of single orange bands ending in one white band down each column. Wrap a white band around your hook twice and stretch it between the seventh middle peg and the fifth right peg. Repeat on the other side. Wrap a black cap band around the seventh middle peg three or four times.

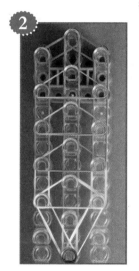

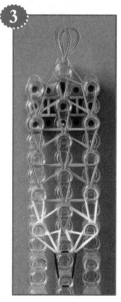

2. Wrap an orange band around your hook twice, and stretch it onto the second row in a triangle shape. Repeat to make four total triangle shapes across your tail, using a white band for the last triangle.

3. Loop your tail shape as usual, looping the middle column then the outside columns.

4. Secure the loose bands with a spare hook and set aside.

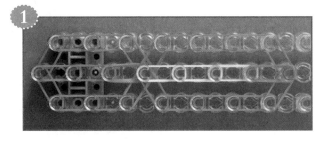

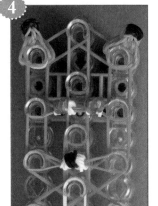

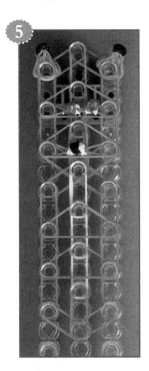

Putting It Together:

1. Use double orange bands to lay out a long hexagon shape for your fox's head. Lay double orange bands down the middle of your hexagon shape. Use double orange bands to lay out a larger hexagon shape for the body. Lay a line of double bands down the middle of the bigger hexagon, starting with white and ending with orange bands.

2. Wrap a black band around your hook four times, then thread it onto two white bands that have been doubled over. This is your snout. Thread the white bands onto a single orange band. Carefully set aside, or place on your spare hook.

3. Wrap a blue band onto your hook four times. Thread it onto a single white band that has been doubled, as you did for the snout. Repeat to make a second eye. Thread both eyes onto a single orange band.

4. Place the single band from your eyes onto the outside pegs in the second row. Place your snout across the third row. Place the ears on the first two pegs on the right and left.

5. Attach a single orange band across the second row in a triangle shape. Repeat in the third row.

Attach double orange bands to the fifth and sixth rows in a triangle shape.

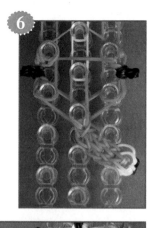

6. Place the tail onto the eighth middle peg. Attach the back legs to the sixth and seventh pegs in the outside columns.

7. Begin looping your fox shape, starting at the peg where you placed the tail. Loop all the bands from that peg, then continue looping the outside pegs until you reach the diagonal neck pegs.

8. Place one of your front legs onto your hook. Loop the diagonal orange off the fourth outside peg, and thread the loops from your leg onto the band before looping it onto the fourth middle peg. Do the same with the other leg on the other side.

9. Loop the rest of the middle pegs in the body shape. Continue looping your fox as usual.

10. Secure the final loose loops with a single orange band. Remove your fox from the loom. You can tuck the tie-off band into the back of your fox's head using your hook.

OWL

Who? Who else but this adorable owl charm! This project has lots of small parts; some are made on the loom, and some are made with your hook. Make sure to pay attention to the written instructions so you don't miss anything!

Difficulty level: **Easy**

You need:

1 loom • 1 hook • gray bands • orange bands •
white bands • blue bands

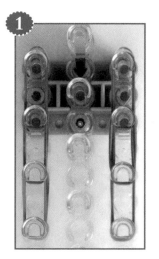

To Make the Wings:

1. Lay a line of double bands down the outside columns, starting on the first and ending on the fourth peg. Use one orange and one gray band per double band. Wrap a single band around the fourth peg on either side three or four times as a cap band.

2. Loop your wings back as usual. Remove from the loom and carefully set aside for now.

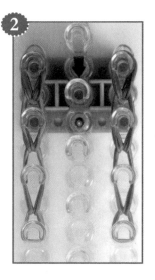

To Make the Body:

1. Using double gray bands, lay out a small hexagon shape onto your loom. Lay a line of double gray bands down the middle of your hexagon.

2. To make the feet, wrap two orange bands around your hook three times, then thread them onto double orange bands. Before looping the end of the double orange bands onto the hook, wrap a single orange band around your hook three times, then loop the end of the double band onto the hook behind it. Thread all the orange bands onto a double gray band. Set it aside for now, and repeat to make a second foot.

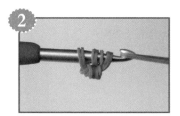

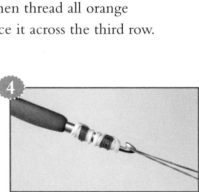

3. Using double gray bands, lay out a longer hexagon shape for your owl's body. For the bottom diagonal bands, place the gray bands from your owl's feet. Lay a line of bands down the middle of your larger hexagon. Use an orange and a gray band for the first double band, then use three gray bands for the next three.

4. To make the eyes, wrap a blue band around your hook four times, then wrap two single white bands around the blue band, twice on either side. Repeat to make the second eye on the hook. Then thread both eyes onto a single gray band. Place across the second row.

5. To make the beak, wrap a single orange band around your hook four times. Then take a double orange band and double it to make it extra tight before threading the single band onto it. Loop both ends of the double orange band onto the hook. Then thread all orange bands onto a single gray band, and place it across the third row.

6. To make the ears, wrap a single gray band around your hook four times. Then thread it onto a doubled gray band. Place the ear onto the first peg on the right, then repeat to make a second and place it on the first peg on the left. Attach your owl's wings to the fourth outside pegs.

7. Place holding bands across your owl shape. Place a single band across the second row in a triangle shape. Repeat across the third, fifth, and sixth rows. Wrap a single band around the last middle peg three or four times as a cap band.

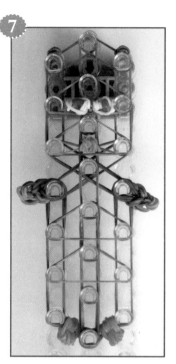

8. Loop your owl shape as usual. Loop the outside pegs up to the neck peg, then loop up the center. Once you have looped the neck peg up to the face, stop. To add extra "poofy cheeks"

to your owl's face, wrap a single gray band around your hook four times, then pick up the band that is looped back to the third peg on the left, and thread the wrapped gray band onto it before putting it back onto the third left peg. Do the same for the third peg on the right. Attach a single orange band to the first pegs on the right and left, then pull the middle over the second middle peg.

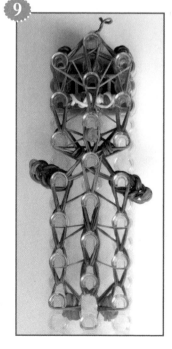

9. Continue looping your owl as usual. Loop the outside pegs of the head shape, then loop the middle pegs. Secure the final loose loops with

a single gray band pulled into a slipknot.
Remove your owl from the loom.

10. To make the tail, wrap three gray bands
    around your hook twice, then attach them
    from the first to the second peg. Wrap two
    gray bands around your hook twice, and
    attach them from the second to the third
    peg. Wrap a single gray band around the
    third peg four or five times as a cap band.

11. Loop your tail back as usual. Thread a single
    gray band through the final loose loops in a
    slip knot. Remove the tail from the loom.

12. To attach the tail to your owl, put your
    hook through a loop in his bottom, then
    pull the single band from the tail through
    the loop. Pull the tail through the single
    gray loop to secure it.

ROCKeT

Ready . . . Liftoff! You will "double" some of your bands in this project, so they are extra tight. Many of the other bands in this project are not doubled, though, so make sure to pay attention to the instructions!

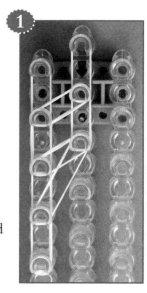

Set up your loom offset, with the middle column pulled one peg up.

To Make the Boosters:

1. Attach a single band from the first to the second peg in the middle and left columns. Continue laying double bands down the left column. Pause on the fourth peg to attach a diagonal double band to the middle column, then continue to the fifth peg. Wrap a cap band around the fifth peg three or four times. Add two doubled bands as holding bands.

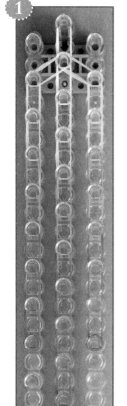

2. Loop your booster shape back. Remove and set aside so that it doesn't unravel. Make four total boosters this way.

To Make the Fire:

1. Double a single white band, then attach it from the first to the second middle peg. Repeat and attach from the second to the third peg. Wrap a yellow band around your hook and attach it from the second middle to the second left peg. Repeat on the right. Continue laying doubled bands down all three columns, starting with yellow, then switching to orange, and finally red bands. Wrap a single red band around each of the end pegs three or four times as a cap band.

2. Wrap a yellow holding band around your hook twice, then attach it across the second row. Repeat to place a yellow holding band across the third row, then orange across the fourth and fifth rows, and red across the sixth row.

3. Loop your fire, starting from the cap bands and working your way back to the start of the loom. Carefully remove your fire and set it aside.

Make the Rocket Top:

1. Lay out doubled red bands from the first to the fourth peg. Wrap a single red band around the fourth peg three or four times as a cap band.

2. Loop your rocket top back as usual. Carefully remove the piece and set it aside so that it doesn't unravel.

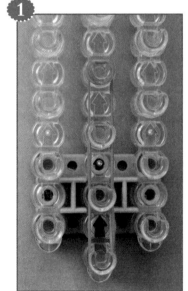

To Make the Rocket Body:

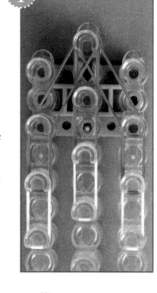

1. Attach two red bands from the first to the second, and another two from the second to the third middle peg. Attach a single red band to the first middle peg and connect it to the second right peg. Repeat on the left side. Attach double red bands from the second to the third outside pegs. Attach double white bands from the third to the fourth peg in all rows.

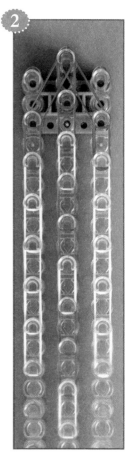

2. Attach three clear blue jelly bands from the fourth to the fifth and fifth to the sixth middle pegs. Attach three white bands from the sixth to the seventh middle peg, then lay down two more sets of three clear blue jelly bands. Attach three white bands from the ninth to the tenth middle peg. Lay a line of white triple bands up the outside columns, from the fourth to the eighth peg.

3. Attach three blue jelly bands from the tenth to the eleventh middle peg. Wrap a white band around your hook twice and attach it to the middle column from the eleventh to the twelfth peg. Repeat and place it on the last two pegs in the column. Lay

double white bands down the outside columns
from the eighth to the second-to-last peg. Attach
three white bands from the second-to-last to the
last peg in the outside columns. Close up your
rocket shape by attaching two white bands from
the last middle peg to the last outside peg, then
repeat on the other side.

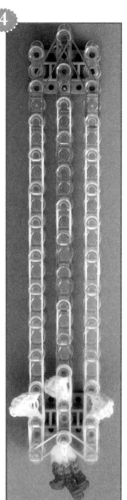

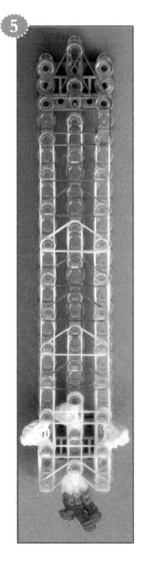

4. Attach your fire to the last
middle peg. Attach two of
your boosters to the third
and second pegs from the
end in the outside columns.
Attach the third booster to
the second and third pegs
from the end in the middle
column: put the piece point-
down and attach the two sets
of loops as you did for the
other two.

5. Attach holding bands. Wrap a
single white band around your hook twice, and
attach it across the second-to-last row on the
loom. Repeat to attach to the next row. Attach
bands in a triangle shape across the rest of the
rows of your rocket: use single blue bands for
the rows where you have placed windows and
double white bands for the non-window rows.
Wrap a red band around your hook twice and
attach it to the third row. Repeat and attach it
to the second row.

6. Attach your last booster piece to the top of the middle column, attaching the two sets of loops to the second and third pegs from the end, with the point facing up.

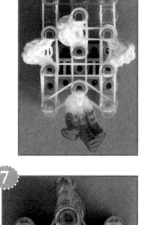

7. Place the rocket top onto the first middle peg.

8. Starting at the last middle peg where you placed your fire piece, begin looping your rocket back. Loop the outside columns, then the middle column. When you reach the booster piece attached to the middle column, make sure to pull the booster piece through the band as you loop it back to the third peg from the end. That way your booster piece will stick out instead of being flattened. Secure the final loose loops with a red single band pulled into a slipknot.

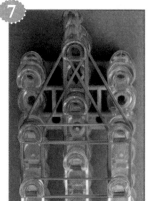

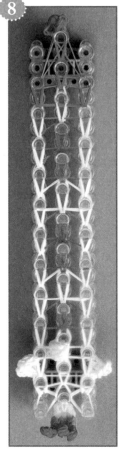

9. Remove your rocket from the loom!

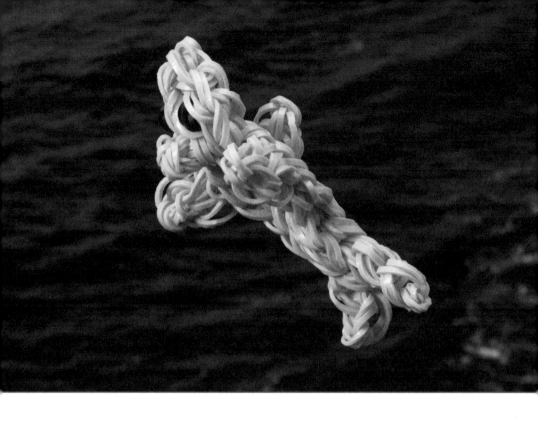

DOLPHIN

Dive into this great project! This fun dolphin makes a delightful friend for your other loom creatures, though we don't promise that he can actually swim.

Difficulty level: **Medium**

You need:

1 loom • 2 hooks • blue bands • white bands

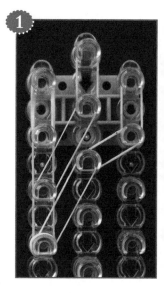

Set up your loom offset so that the center column is one peg farther away from you.

1. Using blue single bands, make the flippers by laying out the figure shown. Note that two of the diagonal bands are stretching the length of two pegs. Attach a cap band to the bottom peg.

2. Attach a triangular holding band across the middle of the fin and a smaller holding band from the third left peg diagonally to the bottom center peg. Both bands are a single band that has been "doubled," or wrapped once on itself.

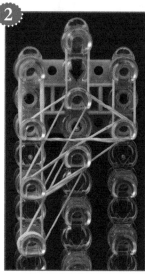

3. Starting from the cap band, loop the bands back to the pegs where they started. Make sure to loop the diagonal bands, but not the holding bands.

4. To make the dorsal fin, you will use a slightly smaller layout than the flippers. Create the shape shown using single blue bands. Attach a cap band to the bottom peg.

5. Connect the second pegs using a single holding band that has been "doubled," or wrapped once on itself.

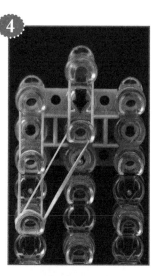

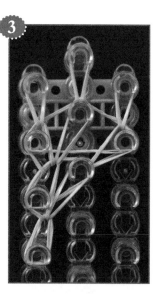

6. Starting from the cap band, loop the bands back to the pegs where they started.

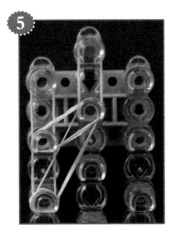

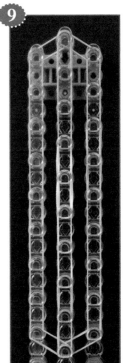

7. To make the eyes, wrap a single black band around your hook several times. To make the whites of the eye, take a single white band and start to wrap it twice around one side of the black bundle, and then finish wrapping on the other side. Repeat this step for the second eye.

8. Slide both eyes onto a single blue band.

9. To make the body of the dolphin, you will be using double bands. Lay out the figure shown, using white bands in the center for the dolphin's belly. Attach the bands on the outside first, followed by the center column.

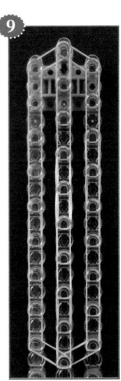

10. Attach the flippers to the outside of the body (from pegs 4, 5, and 6 on both sides). Attach the dorsal fin upside-down from pegs 6 and 7. Attach the eyes and a nose across the face. The nose will just be a single chain with two or three

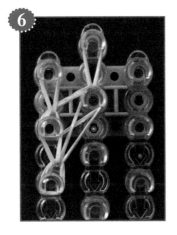

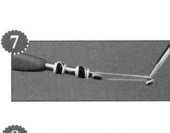

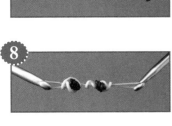

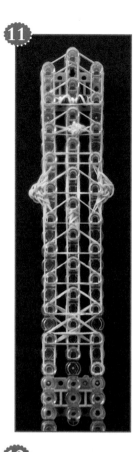

stitches using double bands. At the bottom of the figure, attach two diagonal double bands, and two sets of double bands to the outside columns for the flukes, or the back fin. Finish with a cap band on both.

11. You will now attach holding bands to the body of the dolphin. The top two triangular holding bands will be single bands. The holding band across the fourth row will be a single band that has been "tripled," or wrapped three times on itself. The next two holding bands will be single triangles, followed by two triangular holding bands that have been "doubled" to keep them tight. The final holding band will be a double band, or two bands combined as one.

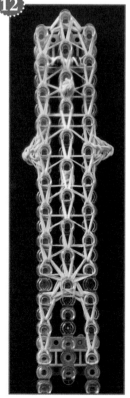

12. Starting from the cap bands, carefully loop all the bands back to the pegs where they started. Loop the outside bands first, then finish with the center column. Secure the top of the project with a c-clip or a rubber band before you take it off the loom.

TULiP

Pretty as a picture, this tulip is so simple and quick that you can make a whole bouquet in no time. These directions are for a small tulip, but if you prefer larger ones, then simply use two rubber bands on every peg, rather than the tight single bands.

Difficulty level: **Easy**

You need:

1 loom • 1 hook • green rubber bands • pink rubber bands (or other color of your choice)

Set up your loom offset so the center 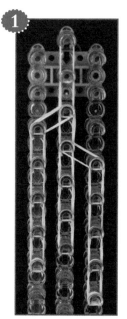 column is one peg farther away from you. All bands will be single bands that have been "doubled," or wrapped once on themselves.

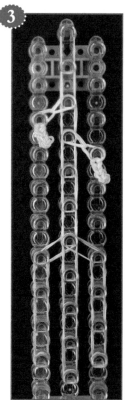

1. Using single green bands that have been "doubled," lay out the shape of the stem. Make sure to lay out the center column first, followed by the two outer columns. Tie off the outer leaves with a cap band.

2. Starting from the cap bands in the outside columns, loop the bands back to the pegs where they started until you reach the center stem.

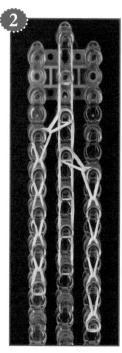

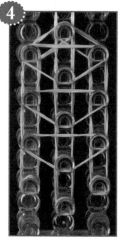

3. Free up the outside columns by detaching the leaves from most of the pegs, but do not remove them completely from the loom. Starting from the end of the stem, lay out the flower shape. Add cap bands to each of the ends of the petals.

4. Add three triangular holding bands to secure the flower. The top triangle will be two pink bands, while the other two will each be single bands that have been "doubled."

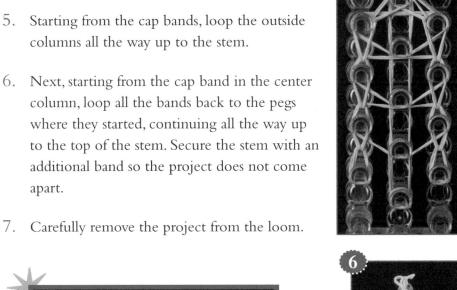

5. Starting from the cap bands, loop the outside columns all the way up to the stem.

6. Next, starting from the cap band in the center column, loop all the bands back to the pegs where they started, continuing all the way up to the top of the stem. Secure the stem with an additional band so the project does not come apart.

7. Carefully remove the project from the loom.

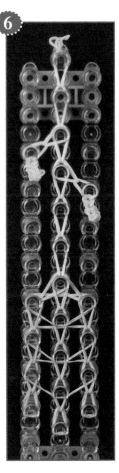

LOCK AND KEY

With this cute little charm, you can show someone special just how you feel about him or her. This makes a fun friendship charm or a gift for a special valentine! Many of these bands are doubled, so be careful when looping!

Difficulty level: **Easy**

You need:

1 loom • 1 hook • yellow bands • red bands • gray bands

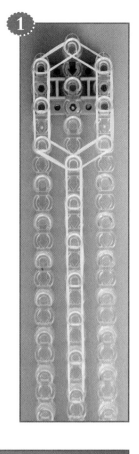

Set up your loom so the center column is one peg away from you.

To Make the Key:

1. Lay down yellow doubled bands in a hexagon shape. Then lay out a line of doubled yellow bands from the fourth to the tenth middle peg.

2. To make the "teeth" of the key, wrap a single yellow band around your hook four times. Then take another single yellow band, double it onto itself, and then thread the looped yellow onto the doubled band. Loop both ends of the band onto the hook. Thread this onto another single yellow band that has been doubled over. Repeat to make two total teeth.

3. To place your "teeth" onto your key, place one onto the last peg, and the second onto the third peg from the end.

4. Loop your key as usual. Secure the final loose loops with a single yellow band pulled into a slipknot.

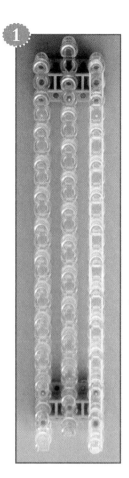

To Make the Lock:

1. Lay a line of doubled yellow bands down the right column until you reach the end. Wrap a single yellow band around the last peg three or four times as a cap band.

2. Loop your yellow chain as usual. Remove from the loom and set aside so that it doesn't unravel.

3. Use double red bands to lay out your lock shape. Attach two red bands from the second middle peg to the first outside peg. Continue laying out double bands to make half a heart shape, then lay out the other half. Wrap a red band around your hook twice and attach it from the second to the third middle peg. Attach two red bands from the third to the fourth middle peg, then attach two gray bands from the fourth to the fifth peg. Wrap a single red band around the last middle peg three or four times as a cap band. Place double red holding bands across the second and third rows. Double the holding band for the fourth row.

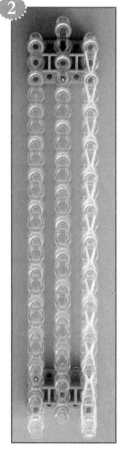

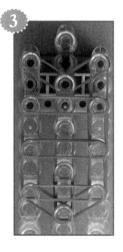

4. Attach your yellow chain from earlier to the first two pegs in the outside columns.

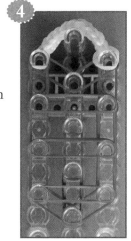

5. Loop your lock as usual. Loop the outside columns first, all the way back to the second middle peg, then loop the middle column. To add more lock detail, wrap a gray band around your hook four times, and when you loop the bands from the fourth to the third peg, thread the looped bands onto the red band before placing it on the peg. Then continue looping as usual. Secure the loose loops with a red band pulled into a slipknot.

SUV

Vrooom! Hit the road with this speedy SUV! Since it uses mostly double bands, this project is sturdier than other projects, making it easy to assemble. Make it in a bunch of colors to make your own gas-guzzling convoy!

Difficulty level: **Easy**

You need:

1 loom • 1 hook • red bands • black bands • yellow bands • gray bands • clear bands • blue bands • white bands

To Make the Wheels:

1. Using double black bands, lay out a pentagon shape, starting at the first and ending on the third middle peg.

2. Attach a single black band to the second middle peg and connect it to the third peg on the right. Continue laying out single bands from the middle peg to the pegs in your pentagon shape, moving in a counterclockwise direction (so you end on the third middle peg). Wrap a red cap band around the middle peg three or four times.

3. Begin looping your "spoke" bands through your cap band and back to the pegs where they started, moving in a clockwise direction (opposite to how you laid them out).

4. Wrap a black cap band around the third middle peg three or four times. Starting at your cap band, begin looping the bands of your pentagon back where they started. Secure the loose loops with a single black band, then remove your wheel from the loom. Repeat to make four total wheels.

To Make the Windows and Roof:

1. Using clear and red double bands, lay out the shape of your windows and roof. Lay out the clear diagonal bands first: this is your windshield. Then lay out the double clear and red bands down all three columns, as shown.

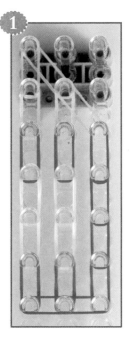

In the seventh row, attach a single red band to each of the outside pegs and connect them to the center peg.

2. Wrap a single band around the second peg in the right column like a cap band, but only wrap it two times. Repeat for the rest of the pegs in the column (skipping the first one). You will use these "connector" bands to attach your car's roof to the body later.

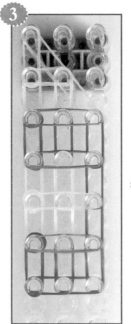

3. Wrap a clear band around your hook twice, then stretch it across the two pegs in the second row. Wrap a red band around your hook twice and place it across all three pegs in the third row. Continue to lay out "holding" bands across the fourth, fifth, and sixth rows, using clear for the fifth row.

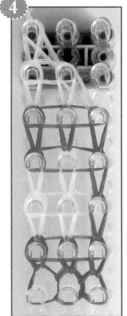

4. Begin looping your shape: start at the last peg in the left column, and loop across the whole row from left to right. Then loop the middle column, followed by the right column. Loop the diagonal clear bands, then finish looping the left column. Secure the loose loops with a single clear band.

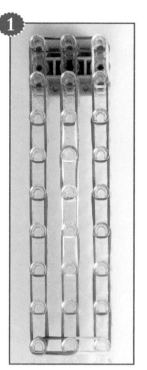

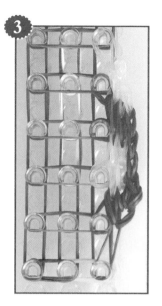

To Make the Car Body:

1. Using double bands, lay out the body shape of your car. Wrap a gray cap band around the left peg on the end three or four times.

2. Double a red band and place it across the second to last row in your car shape. Repeat to lay a "holding" band across each row in your car shape, skipping the first and last rows (where your bumpers and lights are).

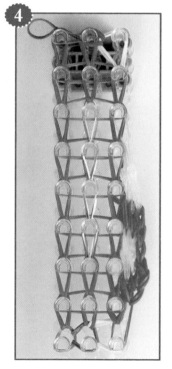

3. Attach your hood and window piece to the loom using the "connector" bands along the outside edge. You will attach it at seven points.

4. Begin looping your car shape, starting on the last peg in the left column, where you placed your cap band. Loop the last row, moving from left to right, then begin looming your right column, where you have attached the top of the SUV. Secure the final loose loops with a single gray band and remove the car from the loom.

5. Use a hook to tuck the end of the gray single band into the car shape. Take up one of your wheel shapes and put your hook through the center. Pull the single black band through the center. Put your hook through your SUV where you would like to put your wheel. Grab the loop from the single black band and pull it through your SUV shape, then open the loop and put the wheel through it to secure it. Put your hook through the same stitch, coming from the side where your wheel is attached, and connect the second wheel to the other side in the same way. Attach the other two wheels.

MONKEY

Go bananas for this monkey project! This fun animal is a great addition to your zoo of charms. Try adding the top hat and making the banana project to make this guy even more fun!

Difficulty level: **Easy**

You need:

1 loom • 1 hook • black bands • white bands • blue bands

Set up your loom offset so that the center column is one peg farther away from you. All bands are double bands, or two bands combined as one.

1. For the arms, lay out five black double bands. Add two separate cap bands to the bottom of the column—this will make him look like he has fingers.

2. Starting from the cap bands, loop the bands back to the pegs where they started. Secure the bands temporarily, remove it from the loom, and set it aside for later. Repeat these steps for a second arm.

3. This next photo shows how to make both the eyes (left) and the ears (right). For the eyes, attach a single white band, a double black band, and a blue cap band. For the ears, attach a black double band and a cap band.

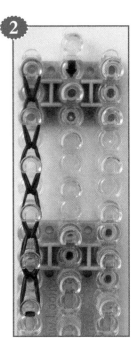

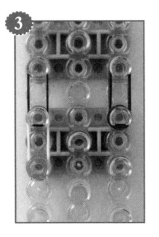

4. Starting from the cap band, loop the bands back to the pegs where they started. Repeat steps 3 and 4 to make the second eye and ear.

5. For the head of the monkey, lay out the hexagon shape shown in black and white double bands. Make sure to put the bands in the center column on after you have put down the hexagon.

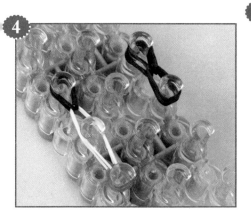

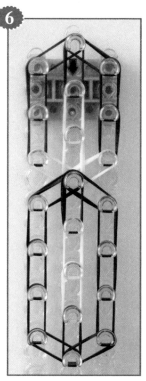

6. Moving down to the torso, create a large hexagon using black and white double bands.

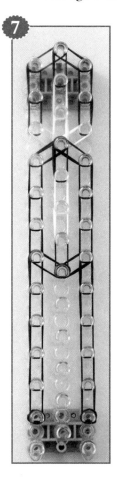

7. Next, attach legs to either side of the monkey. The legs will be five black double bands that are finished off with two separate cap bands on the same peg.

8. Attach two triangular holding bands to the monkey's torso. These are single black bands. Attach the eyes and the ears to the face (both on the second outside pegs), followed by a white and a black holding band.

9. Starting with the feet where you placed your cap bands, begin to loop the bands back to the pegs where they started. Loop the outside columns all the way up

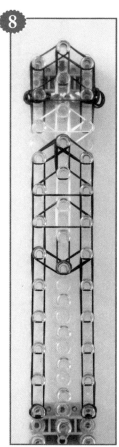

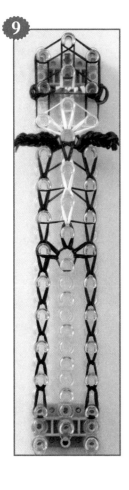

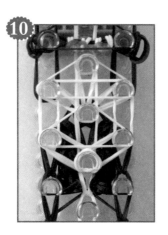

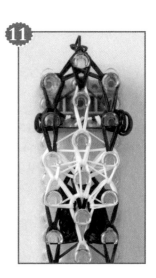

to the tops of the shoulders (the diagonal bands). Here, slide the arms onto the shoulder bands as you are looping them to their pegs. This will keep the arms in place. Do this for both arms, and then loop the center column of the monkey's torso, as well as the white part of his mouth. Stop looping here.

10. Now you will make the big part of the monkey's chin. Push all of the bands and the arms down so they are not in the way, and then start attaching more white bands. First, attach white double bands from the third center peg to the fourth center peg and the from the fourth center peg to the fifth center peg. Take a single white band that has been "doubled" and attach it from pegs 3 to 4 on the left-hand column and another for pegs 3 to 4 in the right-hand column. On each side, take a white double band and attach it diagonally from fourth peg to the fifth center peg. Attach holding bands across the third row, and a single triangular holding band across the fourth row. Attach a cap band to the fifth center peg.

11. Very carefully, loop the rest of these bands back to the top of the monkey's head. Loop the outside columns before the center column, and then secure the project with a rubber band or a c–clip. Gently remove the project from the loom.

SUNGLASSES

Get some shade with these miniature sunglasses! Like the top hat, these sunglasses can be worn by many of our loom creatures. They're also great as a dangling charm for a zipper or necklace! We've chosen to use mostly black bands, but feel free to vary the colors in any way you like.

Difficulty level: **Easy**

You need:

1 loom • 1 hook • black bands • bands in a color of your choice

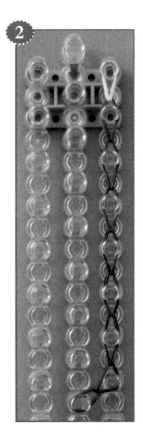

Set up the loom offset so that the center column is one peg farther away from you. All the bands are single bands that have been "doubled," or wrapped once on themselves.

1. First, you will make the sides of the sunglasses. Starting in the right-hand column, lay out a column of "doubled" bands, starting with a bright color and then switching to black. At the eighth peg, connect another "doubled" band diagonally to the center column. Attach a cap band here.

2. From the cap band, loop all the bands back to the pegs where they started, ending at the top of the loom. Secure the top of the project and set aside for later. Repeat these steps for the other side of the sunglasses.

3. Next, turn your loom so that it is horizontal. You will now be laying out the shape of the frames. Using black bands that have been "doubled," 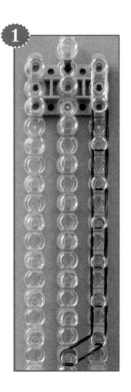 or wrapped once on themselves, attach bands to create the shape shown. Note that the single band that has been attached to the center column was laid out before the hexagons in the sunglasses. Make sure to move from left to right when attaching the bands to the loom.

4. Moving from left to right, attach single bands that have been "doubled" to the center columns in both of the sunglass frames.

5. Attach the two sides of the sunglasses to either side of the frames. Also add four triangular holding bands. These are also single bands that have been "doubled."

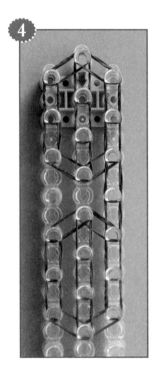

6. Starting from the far right side where you have attached the sides of the glasses, loop your project back. When looping, make sure to loop the far right column (top column if your loom is horizontal) last so that the project stays held together.

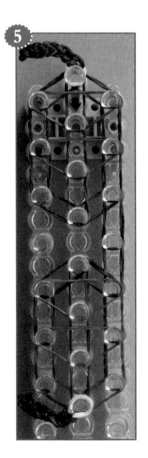

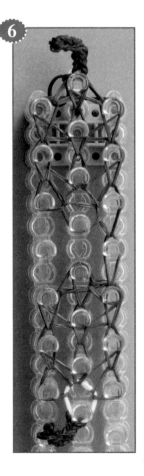

MiTTeNS

Bundle up with your own knitted mittens! Use them as dangly charms to hang from your zipper, add to a bracelet, or attach to earring hooks—these mittens are as cute as can be.

Difficulty level: **Easy**

You need:

1 loom • 1 hook • blue bands • green bands

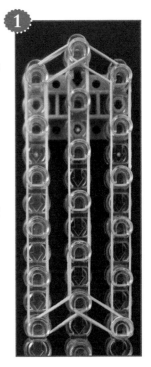

Set up your loom offset so that the center peg is one space farther away from you. All bands are double bands.

1. Lay out your mitten shape, as shown. Notice that the center column has been placed down first, followed by the outer columns. Add your accent colors between pegs 2 and 3 for the outer columns, and between 3 and 4 for the center column.

2. Add three single triangular holding bands to the center of the project and one additional single holding band to the bottom. Note that this last band is a single band that has been "doubled," or wrapped once on itself so that it is taut.

3. For the thumb of your mittens, you will need to do a bit of knitting. Wrap a single band around your hook a few times, and then slide that band onto another double band to create a bundle of bands. Repeat this so you have two bundles as shown in the photo.

4. Using your hooks, slide the outside bands of one bundle onto the outside bands of the other bundle. The piggybacking bands will create the thumb.

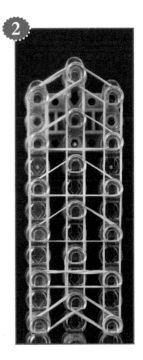

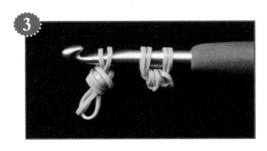

5. Attach the thumb to the loom by the bottom triangular holding band.

6. Loop the project back to the pegs where they started. Make sure to loop the pegs in the center column last.

7. Tie the project off with a rubber band at the top and carefully remove from the loom. Repeat each of these steps for a second mitten.

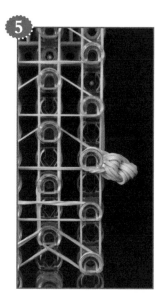

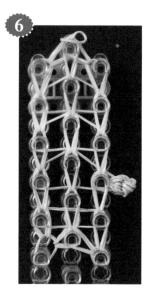

MiGHTY SWORD

Carry a sword like the greatest knights! Luckily, your limbs are safe since the sword is made of rubber. We have added bands to look like gemstones in the hilt of the sword, but feel free to add them wherever you like, or even use real beads. This project is quite simple, but can get tricky when knitting the gems. For extra tips on how to knit, see the glossary at the beginning of the book.

Difficulty level: **Medium**

You need:

1 loom • 2 hooks • gray bands • green bands • blue bands • orange bands

Set up your loom offset so that the center column is one peg further away from you.

1. Using double bands (two bands combined as one), lay out the blade of the sword. Start by placing the bands in the center column first, stopping at the tenth peg down, then attaching the outer columns. Leave a gap between the last band in the center column and the peg where the outer columns connect to the eleventh center peg. Note that all the diagonal bands stretch farther than normal.

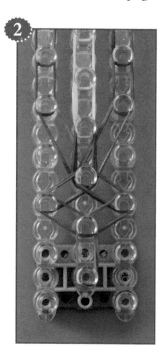

2. Using a gray band, connect the gap in your sword to the peg below where the diagonal bands attach. Next, add gray double bands in a diamond shape to create the center of the guard. Attach an additional gray double band to the last peg in the center column and close it off with a cap band.

3. For the guard of the sword (the two sides that stem outward), you will need to do a little knitting. Start by creating a single chain of lime green bands using single bands that have been "doubled," or wrapped once on themselves. Wrap one of these several times around your hook, then slide it onto another "doubled" band with your hook. Do this another time. For the part with the "gem," wrap

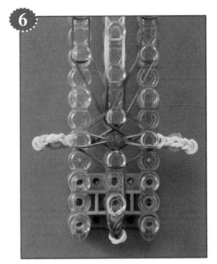

an orange band several times around a second hook and slide it onto another doubled band. Connect this to the bundle you already have by attaching the band with the gem to the first hook, and then sliding one side of the first bundle onto the band with the gem.

4. Remove the side of the band (from the original bundle) that is not connected to the band with the gem, and reattach it to the opposite side of the band with the gem. (You will need to hold the band with the gem with your finger or a hook while you do this.) Your bands should now appear on either side of the orange gem.

5. Finish the rest of this side of the guard of the sword as a normal single chain by adding two more sets of bands. Repeat steps 3 through 5 for a second side of the guard.

6. Attach the guard of the sword to the diamond shape you created. For the gem in the center, simply wrap a blue band around a hook several times and slide it onto a gray double band, attaching the gray band to the sword. For the grip of the sword, repeat the same process as the guard (steps 3 through 5), but vary your colors.

7. Attach eight holding bands to the blade of the sword to hold it together. All these are single bands that have been "doubled," or wrapped once on themselves.

8. Starting from the pommel, or the tip of the handle where you've placed a cap band, loop your band back to the pegs where they started. When you're looping the blade of the sword, loop the outside columns first, and then finish by looping the center column all the way to the top. Secure the top of the project with a band or a c-clip.

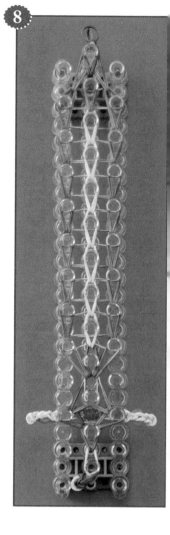

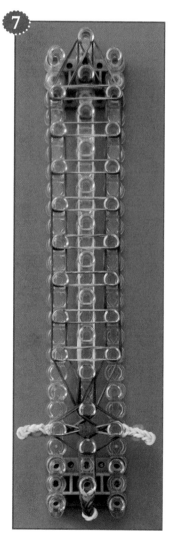

HAPPY HiPPO

King of the river, this hippopotamus is all sorts of fun! This project has a lot of little steps and attachments, so make sure to pay close attention to each. Once you're finished, you'll have one of the coolest animals to add to your loom kingdom!

Difficulty level: **Medium**

You need:

1 loom • 2 hooks • c-clips (optional) • white bands • black bands (or other eye color) • purple rubber bands

Set up your loom offset, with the center
column set one peg away from you.

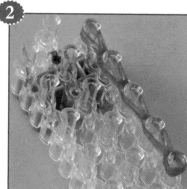

1. Starting with the front legs of the
   hippo, lay out four purple triple bands.
   Instead of a regular cap band, you will
   add three separate cap bands to the last
   peg to make an extra strong cap band.

2. Loop your bands back to the pegs
   where they started. Secure the end of the
   leg with a c-clip, or slide it onto a holding
   hook temporarily. You will use the leg later.

3. Repeat steps 1 and 2 for the second front
   leg and set aside.

4. Repeat step 1. This time, though, add an
   additional triple band between the second
   and third pegs down in the center column.

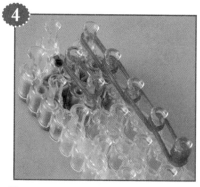

5. Loop your bands back to the pegs where
   they started, with one exception: when
   you reach the middle peg in the column,
   loop the band over to the lone triple band
   in the center column, then loop this band.
   Return to the right-hand column and loop
   the last band, as shown.

6. Secure the ends with a c-clip or slide the
   project onto a hook temporarily. Make
   sure both top loops are secured before
   removing from the loom. Repeat steps 4
   and 5 to make the second hind leg and set
   aside with the other legs.

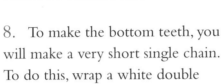

7. To make the hippo's bottom jaw, lay out a pattern of purple double bands, as shown. Note that the first sets of diagonal bands (that go from the second outside pegs to connect to the third center peg) are single bands. The double band that goes from the third to the fourth center pegs should be attached last.

8. To make the bottom teeth, you will make a very short single chain. To do this, wrap a white double band around a hook three times. Attach another white double band to the hook, and slide the first bundle onto it. Reattach the other end of the double bands to create the tooth. Make two and set aside, as shown. For smaller teeth, use single bands.

9. Attach the teeth to the jaw you created. To secure, lay out two holding bands. These are single bands that have been wrapped once on themselves so that they stretch tightly across the loom.

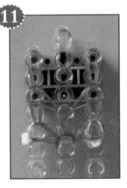

10. Loop the bottom center bands and the diagonal bands back to the pegs where they started, as shown.

11. After, start back at the bottom of your figure and loop the bottom diagonal bands as well as the outside columns. The holding bands stay where they are.

12. Secure this figure with c-clips or by sliding it onto a hook and set aside temporarily.

13. The next figure is the hippo's upper jaw. Lay out the figure shown using purple double bands, starting with the outside columns and then the center column.

14. Repeat step 8 to make the upper teeth. Make two nostrils this same way using single purple bands, but slide these onto a single band that has been wrapped once on itself (making it taut).

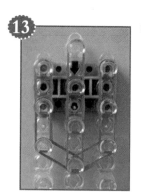 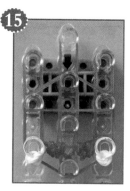  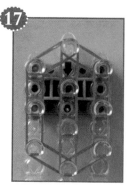

15. Attach the teeth to the figure. To attach the nostrils, stretch the single band holding the nostrils across the loom to connect to the outer columns. Lay out a single holding band in a triangular shape close to the top of the figure.

16. Loop the bands back to the pegs where they started. Begin with the center column, and then move to the outside columns. Secure the top of the project and remove from the loom. You will attach this to the hippo's body later.

17. For the hippo's head, lay out the figure shown using purple double bands. Attach the outside columns first, followed by the center column.

18. For the rest of his body, attach purple double bands for the outer shape. For the center column, use purple triple bands for each of the bands except the last (this will be a double band). The triple bands will make his body bigger.

19. Lay out three double holding bands over the body of the hippo—each will form a triangle. Take the hind legs that you made earlier and attach them to the bottom of the figure. Since there are two loops at the top of each leg, you will use these loops to stretch across two pegs.

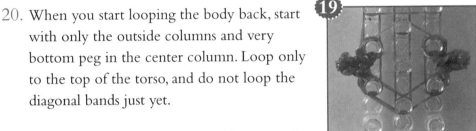

20. When you start looping the body back, start with only the outside columns and very bottom peg in the center column. Loop only to the top of the torso, and do not loop the diagonal bands just yet.

21. To attach the front legs, you will begin as if you are looping the diagonal bands back to the pegs where they started. Before attaching the bands to their original peg, though, slide the leg onto the band, and then attach the band to the peg.

22. Before you loop the hippo's head, you will attach holding bands, ears, and the eyes. Both the ears and the eyes will be made in just the same

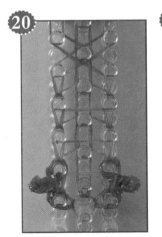

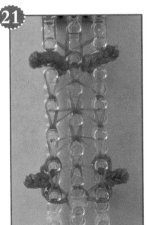

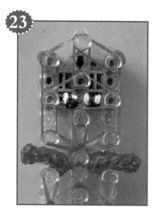

way as the teeth, except you will use different colors. For the eyes, use a single black band and two white bands, and for the ears, use single purple bands. Slide the eyes onto a single purple band and attach this across his face. Attach two single holding bands in triangular shapes over his face, as shown.

23. Next, carefully loop the bottom three bands on the hippo's face, as shown.

24. Attach the bottom of the hippo's jaw to the same area. Push the bands down as far as possible so they don't pop off the loom.

25. Then attach the top of the hippo's mouth to the same area. Since there are three loops that need to attach to the loom, it's easiest to place one section down and loop the bands back to the peg where it started, securing this section of the mouth. Notice how the areas where the mouth is attached are looped back in the photo.

26. Finish looping the rest of the head and secure the top of the hippo's head with a c-clip or a purple double band.

27. Carefully remove the project from the loom. If you'd like to add a tail, create a small chain and attach it to his hindquarters.

SKUNK

This stinker's quick to put together, and he's awfully sweet. His leg bands are doubled, so remember to loop carefully!

Difficulty level: **Easy**

You need:

1 loom • 1 hook • black bands • white bands • blue bands

To Make the Legs:

1. Lay down a line of doubled black bands from the first to the fifth peg. Wrap a single black band around the fifth peg three or four times as a cap band.

2. Loop your black bands back. Remove your chain from the loom and set aside. Repeat to make four total legs.

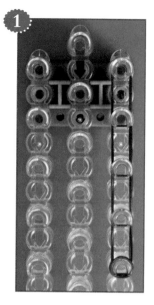

To Make the Tail:

1. Attach two black bands from the first to the second middle peg. Using white single bands, lay out a long hexagon, starting on the second and ending on the seventh middle peg. Lay bands down the middle of your hexagon shape: start with double bands, then three bands from the

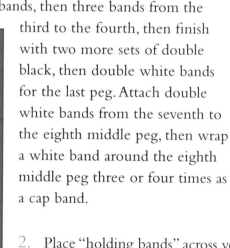

third to the fourth, then finish with two more sets of double black, then double white bands for the last peg. Attach double white bands from the seventh to the eighth middle peg, then wrap a white band around the eighth middle peg three or four times as a cap band.

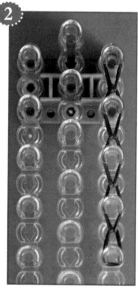

2. Place "holding bands" across your shape by doubling bands and placing them onto the loom in a triangle shape. Repeat to lay four total holding bands up your tail shape.

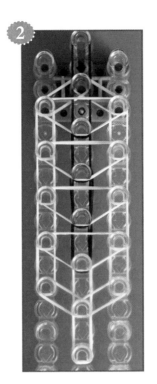

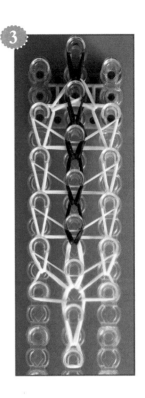

3. Loop your tail, remove it from the loom, and set aside. Secure the loose loops with your hook or a temporary slip knot to keep it from unraveling.

To Make the Body:

1. Lay down a line of double bands from the first to the fourth middle peg: use white for the first two sets, then switch to black. Using black double bands, lay out a hexagon shape.

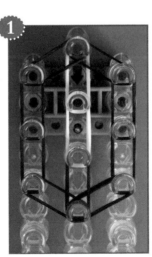

2. Starting at the fourth middle peg and using double black bands, lay out another larger hexagon shape. Lay a line of bands down the center of your larger hexagon: start with two black bands, then switch to double white bands.

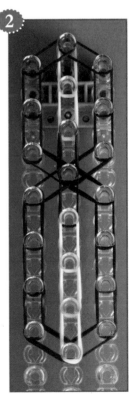

3. To make the eyes, wrap a blue band around your hook four times, then take a single white band and wrap it around the hook four times, so that there are two white loops on either side of the blue band. Repeat to make the second eye on your hook. Then thread both eye pieces onto a single black band. Place it across the second row.

4. To make the snout, wrap a black band around your hook four times, then thread it onto double black bands. Before looping the end of the double black bands back onto your hook, loop a white band three times around the hook. Thread the black and white bands onto a single black band. Set aside, or look ahead to attach your snout to the third row on the loom.

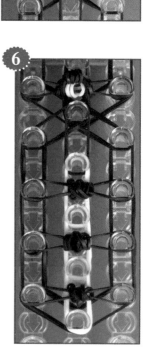

5. To make the ears, wrap a single black band around your hook four times, then thread it onto a single black band doubled over. Repeat to make two ears. Place your ears onto the loom on the first pegs in the outside columns.

6. To make black stripes for your skunk's back, take two black bands and wrap them around your hook three times, then thread them onto a single black band. Place the stripe across the fifth row. Repeat twice more to place three total stripes down your skunk's back.

7. Attach your skunk's tail to the last center peg, and his back legs to the last outside pegs.

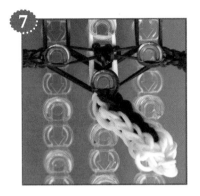

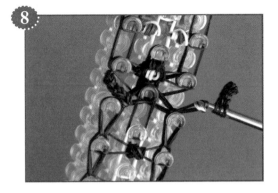

8. Begin looping your skunk shape. Loop the first center peg, then loop up the outside columns until you reach the "shoulder" pegs. To attach the front legs, place a leg on your hook, then when looping the outside peg to the neck peg, thread the leg onto the band before placing it onto the neck peg.

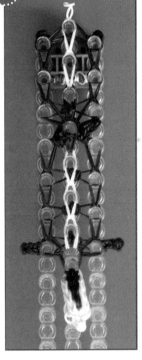

9. Loop up the middle pegs of your skunk's back, then continue looping the skunk shape as usual. Secure the loose loops with a single band pulled into a slip knot.

DRAGONFLY

Fly away with this fun project! Try using glow-in-the-dark bands for the wings for an extra cool dragonfly that lights up at night!

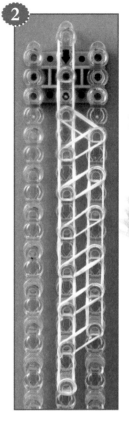

Set up your loom offset so that the center column is one peg farther away from you.

1. For the wings, lay out the figure shown, starting with the center column and then branching out to the right-hand column. These will be single bands that have been "doubled," or wrapped once on themselves. Attach a cap band at the bottom of the figure.

2. Attach five holding bands to secure the wing. These are single bands that have been "doubled."

3. Starting from the cap band at the bottom of the wing, loop the bands back to the pegs where they started until you reach the top of the wing.

4. Repeat these steps to create four total wings.

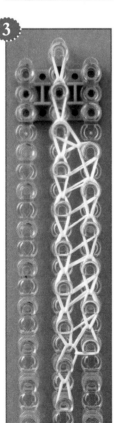

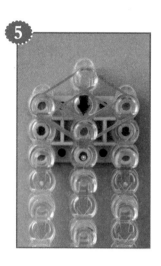

5. Using blue bands, create the head of the dragonfly. These will be double bands, or two bands that are used at the same time.

6. Place a teal double band down the center of the head. Create a hexagon shape for the thorax (the next part of the body) using teal double bands.

7. Attach two double bands down the center of the body.

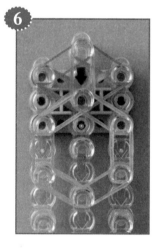

8. At the bottom of the thorax, lay out the long part of the abdomen using double bands for seven rows. We alternated using pink, teal, and blue colors, but you can use whatever colors you like. Attach a cap band at the bottom of the project.

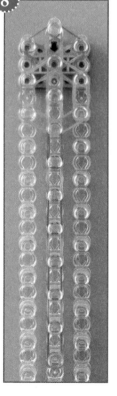

9. To create the eyes, take a black band, a blue band, and a lime green band and wrap them several times around your hook. Do this again for a second eye, and then slide them onto a single blue band.

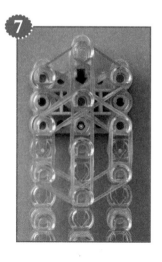

10. Stretch this single band to attach the eyes to the top outside pegs in the head. Attach a single teal holding band to the thorax to hold the project in place.

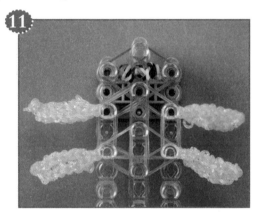

11. Connect the four wings to the four pegs in the thorax, as shown.

12. Starting with the bottom of the dragonfly, loop the bands back up all the way to the top of the dragonfly's head. Be careful not to skip bands or go out of order. Attach two rubber bands to the top of the project to secure it. These can also be the dragonfly's antennae.

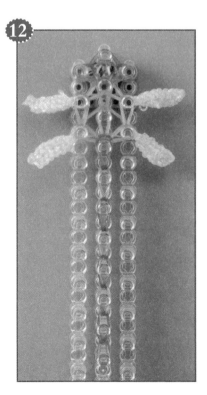

LiON

Get ready to roar with your loom lion! This king of the jungle requires a lot of bands for his mane, so just be careful when you are looping the project back to keep all of them secure. We chose orange and yellow bands for this project, but you can try out different shades, or even make his mane rainbow-colored!

Difficulty level: **Medium**

You need:

1 loom • 2 hooks • yellow bands • orange bands •
black bands • white bands

Set up your loom offset so that the center column is one peg farther away from you. All bands will be double bands.

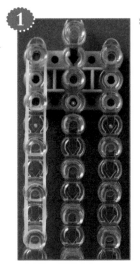

1. To make the legs, you will set up a single chain on your loom. Lay out four yellow double bands and finish with a cap band on the last peg.

2. Starting from the cap band, loop the bands back to the pegs where they started. Secure the top of the leg on a holding hook or with a temporary c–clip and set aside. Repeat steps 1 and 2 for the second leg.

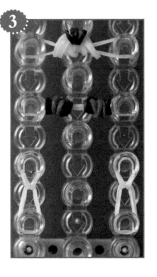

3. Next you will create the nose, eyes, and ears. For the nose, wrap a yellow double band around your hook several times. Slide this onto a single yellow band to create a small bundle. Wrap a single black band around your hook several times. Slide this onto a yellow double band. Slide this bundle onto the first bundle—you will need to switch between hooks as if you are knitting. For the eyes, wrap a single blue band around your hook several times, then wrap the first half of a black band on one side of

the blue band, and then finish on the other. Repeat this for the second eye and then slide both eyes onto a single yellow band. For the ears, attach a single yellow band to your loom and finish it with a cap band. Loop this band back to its original peg. Set all these aside for later.

4. To make the lion's head and mane, you will create a hexagon of yellow double bands, as shown in the photo. Before attaching the bands to the loom, slide five or six orange bands over the yellow bands, then attach the yellow bands to the loom.

5. In the center of the mane, attach two more bands down the center column. These bands will also have five or six orange bands over them as well before you attach them to the loom.

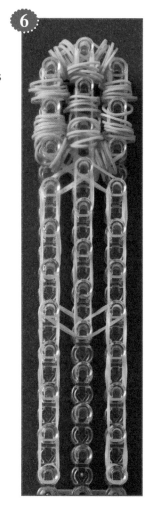

6. To make the body of the lion, attach a large hexagon to your loom, but continue down four additional pegs on the outside columns for the legs. Finish those columns with cap bands. Fill in the center of the belly *after* you have laid out the hexagon of the lion's belly. If you'd like, switch to orange bands in the center of the lion's torso. Place a cap band at the bottom peg in the center column where the torso ends.

7. Attach the ears to the first pegs in the outside columns, attach the eyes to the second pegs in the outside columns, and attach the nose to the third pegs in the outside columns. Attach two

triangular holding bands to the center of the lion's belly.

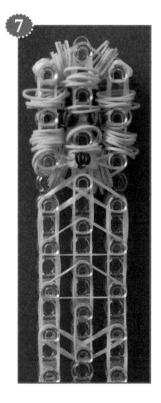

8. On the second and third outside pegs, add four or five more orange bands for the mane, and hold them in place with triangular holding bands, as shown.

9. Starting from the cap bands at the bottom of the legs, begin to loop your project back to the pegs where they started. Loop the outside columns first until you reach the shoulder bands, or just before the mane starts. As you are looping these diagonal bands, slide the arms onto the bands and finish looping it onto the center peg. Loop the center column of the belly up to the peg just before the mane to secure everything.

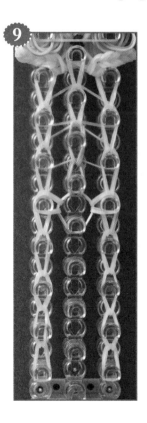

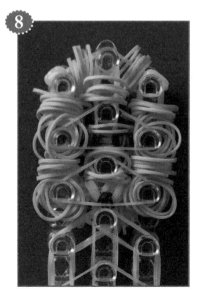

10. Carefully loop the face and mane back. There are a lot of bands, so you may need to use another hook to fish your way to the bands that need to be looped. Loop the outside columns before the center column, and add additional orange bands to the three pegs at the top to make the mane bigger.